D1190384

WILD
EARTH
SCIENCE

WILDFIRES

by Jaclyn Jaycox

PEBBLE
a capstone imprint

Published by Pebble, an imprint of Capstone
1710 Roe Crest Drive, North Mankato, Minnesota 56003
capstonepub.com

Library of Congress Cataloging-in-Publication Data
Names: Jaycox, Jaclyn, 1983- author.
Title: Wildfires / by Jaclyn Jaycox.
Description: North Mankato, Minnesota : Pebble, [2022] | Series: Wild earth science | Includes bibliographical references and index. | Audience: Ages 5-8 | Audience: Grades K-1 |
Summary: "Smoke in the air. Crackling wood. Wildfire! Get to safety, fast. Dry weather, strong winds, and careless actions can all cause forests to burn. Firefighters battle wildfires from the ground and from above. But you can be prepared! Learn about wildfires and how to prevent them, pay attention to warnings, and stay safe"—Provided by publisher.
Identifiers: LCCN 2021042207 (print) | LCCN 2021042208 (ebook) |
  ISBN 9781663976963 (hardcover) | ISBN 9781666327557 (paperback) |
  ISBN 9781666327564 (pdf) | ISBN 9781666327588 (kindle edition)
Subjects: LCSH: Wildfires—Juvenile literature.
Classification: LCC SD421.23 .J39 2022 (print) | LCC SD421.23 (ebook) |
DDC 634.9/618—dc23
LC record available at https://lccn.loc.gov/2021042207
LC ebook record available at https://lccn.loc.gov/2021042208

Editorial Credits
Editor: Ericka Smith; Designer: Tracy Davies; Media Researcher: Svetlana Zhurkin; Production Specialist: Katy LaVigne

Image Credits
Associated Press: Marcio Jose Sanchez, 22, The Colorado Springs Gazette/Michael Ciaglo, 23; Getty Images: Ariel Skelley, 24, Daniel Schwedhelm, 15, John Crux Photography, 18, Robert E. Daemmrich, 26; Shutterstock: Andrew Babble, 27, Brais Seara, 9, Christian Roberts-Olsen, 1, 4, DedMityay, 8, dynamic (map background), back cover and throughout, Elizabeth A. Cummings, 12, Erkki Makkonen, 6, Igor Klyakhin, 16, J. Emilio Flores, 20, Jaden Schaul, 19, Joshua Resnick, 29, Natalia Bratslavsky, 17, Neil Lockhart, 13, pashabo, cover (logo), rck_953, 21, Roger Brown Photography, 25, Roman Mikhailiuk, 7, stockpexel, cover, 3, Webb Show, 5; U.S. Fish and Wildlife Service: 11

TABLE OF CONTENTS

Words in **bold** are in the glossary.

UP IN SMOKE!

The sky glows orange. Dark smoke floats toward the sky. It sounds like a train is roaring through the forest. People and animals leave their homes. What is happening? A wildfire!

Smoke from a wildfire covers Portland, Oregon.

A wildfire is a natural disaster. It moves quickly. It can destroy anything in its path. Huge wildfires can also affect the air—and not just near the wildfire. Smoke can travel very far away.

WHAT ARE WILDFIRES?

Wildfires are large, unplanned fires. Most are started accidentally by humans. Burning **ash** from campfires can float away. It can start a fire in another place.

Lightning can also cause wildfires. It strikes about 8 million times a day. Sometimes lightning strikes the ground. If it hits a dry area, it can start a wildfire. Lightning has caused wildfires in Northern California and British Columbia, Canada.

Downed power lines can cause wildfires too.

Wildfires happen in areas like forests and grasslands. They can spread quickly. In a forest, they usually travel about 6 miles (9.7 kilometers) per hour. They move about twice as fast in grasslands.

Wind spreads fire much faster. Wildfires also move faster uphill than downhill when it's windy. Winds blowing uphill fan the flames. The plants ahead of the flames heat up. They light easily when the fire reaches them.

Wildfires are dangerous. You can't predict when one will start. Guessing where they will spread can be hard too. But scientists can predict where and when they are likely to happen.

Some wildfires can be helpful. Dead plants and leaves pile up on forest floors. A fire clears them away. The soil becomes healthier. New plants can grow. Many animals eat plants. They will have more food.

New plants grow after a wildfire in Alaska.

WILDFIRES AND WEATHER

Wildfires can make their own storms. The hot air rises. It carries smoke upward. As the air rises, it cools. Water droplets form. This makes a cloud. Big fires can make big clouds. Sometimes they turn into storm clouds.

Clouds form over a wildfire in California.

Rain can help put the fire out. But these storms can also bring lightning. And lightning can start more fires.

Wildfires can make their own wind too. The hot air rises quickly. This creates a **vacuum**. It sucks in air near the ground. The air is pulled into the center of the fire.

The winds may start to **rotate**. This causes a **fire whirl**, or fire tornado. Some can get as big as a regular tornado. Fire whirls can send burning **debris** and ash flying.

WHERE IN THE WORLD?

Wildfires can happen anywhere. But places experiencing a **drought** have a higher risk. During a drought, rain doesn't come. Plants die. They dry up. This makes it a perfect time for fires.

Wildfires have been worse recently. Our planet is warming up. Droughts are happening more often. This puts more areas at risk.

From 2019 to 2020, Australia experienced its worst wildfires in history. The fires lasted nine months. About 71,875 square miles (186,155 square kilometers) burned. More than a billion animals died. And the fires destroyed more than 3,000 homes.

Wildfires in Australia

A home in Calfornia destroyed by a wildfire in 2020

The United States also had record-breaking wildfires in 2020. There were more than 58,000 wildfires. About 15,625 square miles (40,469 sq km) burned. In California alone, wildfires damaged about 10,500 buildings.

PUTTING OUT FIRES

Wildfires can be hard to put out. They can burn one acre (4,047 square meters) every five seconds. Some firefighters work on the ground to control the fire. Others fly planes over the fire. The planes drop water and **chemicals**. The chemicals help to slow the spread. Large fires can take months to put out.

A plane dropping chemicals on a wildfire

A mudslide after a wildfire in California

Even after firefighters put out wildfires, the damage might continue. Trees and plants help hold soil in place. When wildfires destroy them, soil can easily move. Heavy rain after a fire can cause **landslides**.

Flash floods can happen too. The burned ground can't take in water. The water runs off into rivers and streams. They can quickly overflow. Nearby homes and businesses may flood too.

A truck moved by a flash flood after a wildfire

STAYING SAFE

Wildfires will happen. But there are some things we can do to help **prevent** them. Don't play with matches. Never leave a campfire that's burning. Share what you know with family and friends.

There are also things you can do to stay safe. Be prepared before a wildfire happens. Have an emergency kit ready. Make sure your smoke alarms work. If you smell smoke, cover your mouth and nose with a mask.

You should also pick up leaves and sticks in your yard. They could catch fire if a wildfire is nearby.

You don't need to be near the fire to be affected. The smoke from a wildfire can travel far. It can make it hard to breathe.

If a wildfire gets close, shut your windows. This will help keep the smoke out. Listen to the radio or TV for updates. You may have to leave. Don't return until it is safe.

Whether you're near a wildfire or not, stay alert and stay safe!

GLOSSARY

ash (ASH)—a powder that results from something burning

chemical (KEH-muh-kuhl)—a substance used in or produced by chemistry; medicines, gunpowder, and food preservatives all are made from chemicals

debris (duh-BREE)—the pieces of something that has been broken or destroyed

drought (DROWT)—a long period of weather with little or no rainfall

fire whirl (FYR WURL)—spinning hot air and gas moving upward carrying smoke, flames, and debris

flash food (FLASH FLUHD)—a flood that happens with little or no warning, often during periods of heavy rainfall

landslide (LAND-slyd)—a large mass of earth and rocks that suddenly slides down a mountain or hill

prevent (prih-VENT)—to keep from happening

rotate (ROH-tate)—to spin around

vacuum (VAK-yoom)—space that is completely empty of all matter, including air and other gases

READ MORE

London, Martha. *Wildfires*. Minneapolis: Pop!, 2019.

Maurer, Tracy Nelson. *The World's Worst Wildfires*. North Mankato, MN: Capstone, 2019.

Stark, Kristy. *Dealing with Wildfires*. Huntington Beach, CA: Teacher Created Materials, Inc., 2019.

INTERNET SITES

Kiddle: "Wildfire Facts for Kids"
kids.kiddle.co/Wildfire

Smokey Bear: "Preventing Wildfires"
smokeybear.com/en/smokey-for-kids/preventing-wildfires

Weather Wiz Kids: "Wildfires"
weatherwizkids.com/?page_id=94

INDEX

ABOUT THE AUTHOR

Jaclyn Jaycox is a children's book author and editor. When she's not writing, she loves reading and spending time with her family. She lives in southern Minnesota with her husband, two kids, and a spunky goldendoodle.